How to Build a Wildlife P...

...es

Contents

What sort of garden space have you got?

Does it look like this?

A garden

Or this?

A backyard

Or this?

A balcony

Or this?

A patio garden

Or this?

A window box

Whatever sort of garden you've got, you can turn it into a paradise for wildlife! You can make a nature reserve of your very own – and it needn't cost any money!

How to make a log-pile habitat

You can easily make a log-pile **habitat**. It won't take up much space. Put it into a corner, where it can hardly be seen. Build it somewhere where the wildlife won't be disturbed.

WHAT YOU NEED:

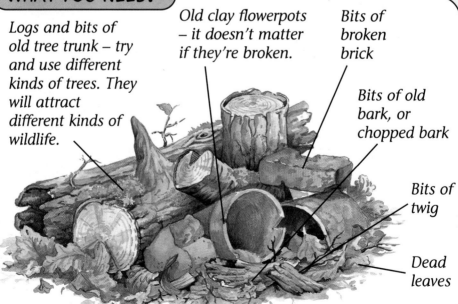

Logs and bits of old tree trunk – try and use different kinds of trees. They will attract different kinds of wildlife.

Old clay flowerpots – it doesn't matter if they're broken.

Bits of broken brick

Bits of old bark, or chopped bark

Bits of twig

Dead leaves

WHAT YOU DO:

All you need to do is heap these things together.

Try to lean them up against a wall or put them near a fence. Ground that is damp is very good for log-pile habitats.

Wait for a bit and watch the wildlife move in.

A log-pile habitat can fit into any garden.

What kind of wildlife will we get in the log-pile habitat?

Blackbirds, thrushes and wrens, looking for food

Hedgehogs, **hibernating** under dead leaves

Earwigs and ground beetles, keeping safe

Woodlice and millipedes, looking for a home under the damp bark

Spiders, making lots of webs

Snails and slugs, hiding from **predators**

Voles, building nests amongst the logs

We might even have toads and frogs hopping in from ponds in nearby gardens, if we're lucky!

7

How to make a butterfly garden

You can build a butterfly garden in a small corner. As long as you have the right kinds of plants, the butterflies will keep flying in, all through the summer.

WHAT YOU NEED:

Compost

Seeds or seedlings from any of these:

Foxglove

Californian poppy

Marigolds

Sweet William

Wallflowers

Candytuft

Honesty Honeysuckle

MULTI PURPOSE COMPOST

Plant pots

WHAT YOU DO:

You can buy seeds or ask for seeds from people who already have these flowers in their garden.

Fill the plant pots with compost and plant the seeds in them.

Water them regularly to keep them growing.

When the seedlings are big enough, plant them in your garden.

Butterflies will come and feed on the nectar in the flowers.

Wall Brown

Red Admiral

Painted Lady

Comma

Cabbage White

Small Tortoiseshell

Brimstone

Common Blue

How to grow a 'butterfly tree'

A buddleia plant attracts lots of butterflies.

WHAT YOU NEED:

Find someone who already has a buddleia and ask them to give you a **cutting** from it.

WHAT YOU DO:

Hold the cutting. Peel off a new side stem with a heel (a piece of the old stem).

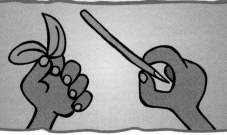

If your bit of stem has any leaves or buds on it, break them off carefully. This makes sure the plant will put all its strength into growing roots.

Poke your cuttings into a pot of compost and water them.

Cover the pot with a plastic bag and hold it down with a rubber band. Take the bag off after a few days.

Keep the pot on your windowsill. Watch your cutting begin to grow.

As the cuttings get bigger, choose the strongest one and plant it in a bigger pot. Look after it until it is strong enough to go outside.

Plant it in the ground, or keep it in a pot. Make sure you water it when it gets dry.

Buddleia grows very quickly. You will soon have a beautiful flowering buddleia – a butterfly tree!

How to make a haven for birds

It's easy to encourage birds into small gardens, even without any trees or bushes.

WHAT YOU NEED:

Some stones

An old dustbin lid, or something of that shape

An old tray

Some nylon cord

WHAT YOU DO:

Make a bird bath

Place the dustbin lid upside down on the lawn or on some paving slabs. If you have a balcony, balance the lid on something.

Make the dustbin lid safe by putting big stones underneath to stop it rocking.

Put some water in it for the birds to drink and bathe in.

Make a bird table

If you are going to hang the bird table up, make holes in the four corners of the tray, thread the cord through and knot it underneath. You can then hang the tray from a tree branch.

If you haven't got a tree, just put the tray out on upturned plant pots, or across the corners of a balcony, or on something like a table.

What about cats?

Put things where cats can't reach them!

13

What food shall we put on the bird table?

We can put all kinds of scraps out for the birds.

WHAT YOU NEED:

Scraps that birds like:

cereal
grated cheese
crumbled bread
bacon fat

bits of fruit   peanuts
cooked rice

You will also need:

string

An empty yoghurt pot

Try to keep the bird table clean. Wash it and wipe it with disinfectant to keep germs away.

WHAT YOU DO:

Make a bird mix

Make a mixture of melted lard or suet and scraps that birds like. Tip it into the yoghurt pot. Wait till it has gone hard, then hang the pot up with a piece of string.

Once we start feeding the birds, they will rely on us for food, so we must carry on.

When their eggs hatch out in spring we must be careful not to feed peanuts or anything too hard. Hard foods can make baby birds choke.

We could grow some plants that have lots of berries. The berries will help to keep lots of birds alive over the winter.

How to make a wetland habitat

Even a very small wetland area can provide a home for all kinds of pond animals.

WHAT YOU NEED:

Water

Sand

A bucket of mud and water from a friend's pond

Stones

Some old bricks

Bits of old drainpipe

Water plants

A sheet of PVC plastic

Some old cloth or carpet

WHAT YOU DO:

If the sides of the pond are too steep hedgehogs can fall in and drown.

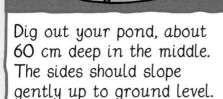

Dig out your pond, about 60 cm deep in the middle. The sides should slope gently up to ground level.

Put sand on the bottom and round the edges to protect your plastic sheeting from sharp stones.

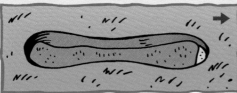

Line the bottom of your pond with the old cloth or carpet.

Lay the plastic sheeting carefully in the hole and up the sides.

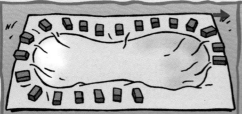

Put the bricks on the plastic, at the edges, to stop it sliding into the pond.

At the bottom of the pond put the stones. Lay the bits of drainpipe on their side at the bottom as well.

Put water in it, but don't fill it to the top. If you fill it up and it then rains, the pond will flood.

Tip in the muddy water from your friend's pond.

If you can get some pond plants from a garden centre or a friend's pond, put them in too.

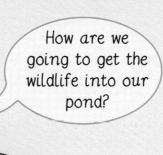

How are we going to get the wildlife into our pond?

There will be lots of wildlife in the mud from the other pond. When they come to drink, birds will bring larvae and seeds on their feet and in their beaks. Toads, frogs and newts may visit to lay their eggs.

Useful things to know about wetland habitats

- Don't put goldfish in your pond. They will eat pond insects.

- Float a small ball in the pond. If the pond freezes over, this will allow the pond life to get the oxygen it needs.

- The best time to build a pond is April or May, because that is when most pond animals are ready to have their young.

- Never take plants from a pond in a local park. Ask your friends to give you some from their own garden pond.

Making a pond, even a very small one, is the best thing you can do for wildlife in your garden. Birds will come to drink at the edge. Insects will like to live there, and frogs and toads will come back year after year to lay their eggs.

Heron, looking for fish to eat

Dragonfly nymph, hatching out

Freshwater shrimp, eating decaying plants

Great diving beetle, looking for tadpoles to eat

Dragonfly, flying in to lay eggs

Mayfly, laying eggs

Mosquito larvae, living under the water before they hatch out

Water boatman, eating worms and insects

Pond snail, eating pondweed

How to make a meadow

It's so easy to build a meadow, you can do it anywhere!

WHAT YOU NEED:

Wildflower seed mix from garden shops
Wild flowers, such as:

Brambles

Buttercups

Nettles

Wild grass

Thistles

Daisies

Dandelions

WHAT YOU DO:

• The easiest way of all to build a meadow is to sprinkle wildflower seed mix on the lawn and leave it to grow wild.

• If you have a big garden, you could mark out part of the garden to be your wild-flower garden, or meadow.

• If you have a small patch, you can simply leave it to see which plants grow there.

• Don't do any weeding, just let the meadow happen.

You can grow wildflower seed mix in an old bucket or a window box. This will make a mini meadow that will attract lots of minibeasts. Sow your seeds in September and they will grow in the spring.

Useful things to know about meadows

• Meadows grow best in poor soil, so do not feed your plants.

• When you cut your meadow, clear all the clippings away. If you leave them lying about they will rot down and make the soil richer, but this not what you want.

And what kinds of wild flowers will grow?

Meadow buttercup

Yarrow

Timothy grass

Knapweed

Meadow foxtail

Speedwell

Red clover

Meadow cranesbill

Plantain

White clover

Never pick wild flowers or dig them up because this will make the meadow disappear. But if there are lots and lots of wild flowers and they have plenty of seed pods, you could take just a few seeds to grow at home.

How to make a woodland habitat

With lots of help, and lots of space, we might be able to build a woodland habitat.

WHAT YOU NEED:

A tree **sapling**

Stake

Ties from the garden shop

Flowers

Logs and bits of old tree trunk

Shrubs

Spade   Fork

Compost

A bucket of water

A sheet of corrugated iron

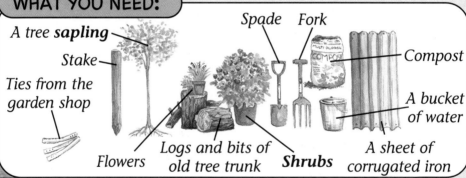

Tits

Toadstools

Worms   Earwigs

WHAT YOU DO:

To plant your tree

1 Plant it between October and March.

2 Plant it at the bottom of the garden.

3 Put the sapling in a bucket of water to give the roots a good drink.

4 Dig a hole deep enough to come just above the roots.

5 Put some compost into the bottom of the hole.

6 Stick in the stake and make it firm.

7 Put the sapling into the hole; hold it carefully while you fill in the soil.

8 Use a tie to hold the sapling to the stake.

To build the rest of your woodland

• Plant the shrubs quite close to the tree.

• Plant the flowers around the outside of your space.

• Make a log-pile habitat (see page 4) with the logs and the tree trunk, in a corner of your space.

• Lay the corrugated iron flat on the soil or grass in another corner to make an underground habitat.

To attract bats to your garden, you could make a bat box and hang it from the tree when the tree is strong enough.

Sparrows

Squirrels

27

Things you need to know

Your wildlife habitats will conserve the natural world, so you can call yourself a conservationist. There are important things that all conservationists need to know.

- You need to know what kind of animal you can find in each habitat. This is because every habitat needs to:

  – feed the animals that live there

  – keep them as safe from predators as possible

  – protect them from bad weather conditions

  – give them a place to have their babies

- You need to learn about **food chains**. Every animal needs food to give it energy to keep it alive and make it grow.

Here are some food chains:

Sun shines, grass grows.   *Slug eats grass.*   *Hedgehog eats slug.*

Sun shines, grass grows.

Caterpillar eats grass.

Blue tit eats caterpillar.

Sun shines, grass grows.

Rabbit eats grass.

Fox eats rabbit.

- You need to know about **life cycles**. Every creature has a different life cycle.

This is the life cycle of a butterfly:

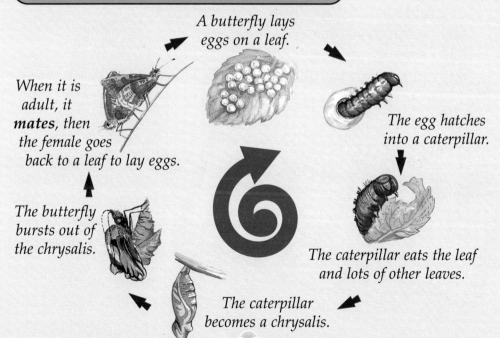

A butterfly lays eggs on a leaf.

*When it is adult, it **mates**, then the female goes back to a leaf to lay eggs.*

The egg hatches into a caterpillar.

The butterfly bursts out of the chrysalis.

The caterpillar eats the leaf and lots of other leaves.

The caterpillar becomes a chrysalis.

How to keep a wildlife diary

WHAT YOU NEED:

A ring binder
Sheets of A4 paper
Four coloured sheets

Pencil
Felt pens
Camera, if possible

WHAT YOU DO:

1 Use the coloured paper to divide your diary into four sections, one for each season: spring, summer, autumn, winter.

2 Use one page for each creature.

Draw a detailed diagram of the creature and write about it.

NOVEMBER

JULY

Keep your diary for at least a year to see how things change over the seasons.

Make sure you write a caption.

Take a photograph and put it in.

Glossary

conservationist   someone who helps keep the natural environment from harm

conserve   to keep from harm

cutting   a piece cut from a plant in order to grow another one

food chain   a series of animals and plants that rely on each other for food

habitat   natural home of a plant or animal

hibernate   to sleep over the winter

life cycle   the natural way for an animal or plant to live, from being born, to having babies, to dying

mate   when animals produce young

nectar   a sweet liquid produced by plants

predator   animal that preys on others

sapling   a young tree

shrub   a woody plant, smaller than a tree, usually with more than one stem

Index